Original title:
Loving Intentionally

Copyright © 2024 Swan Charm
All rights reserved.

Author: Liisi Lendorav
ISBN HARDBACK: 978-9916-89-598-6
ISBN PAPERBACK: 978-9916-89-599-3
ISBN EBOOK: 978-9916-89-600-6

Echoes of Authentic Connection

In the silence, hearts entwine,
Whispers soft as dreams divine.
Eyes that meet, the world stands still,
Moments cherished, hearts fulfill.

Laughter weaves a gentle thread,
Stories shared, the paths we tread.
Hands that clasp in trust so deep,
Echoes of the love we keep.

Crafting a Love Story with Intention

With every word, a seed is sown,
In gardens where our love has grown.
Chapters penned with open hearts,
Together, life's sweet art imparts.

Every glance, intent refined,
In the canvas, love aligned.
Brushstrokes dance in colors bright,
Crafting dreams that take to flight.

The Dance of Conscious Embrace

In twilight's glow, our spirits sway,
A dance of souls, come what may.
With tender moves, we find our way,
In rhythms that forever play.

Breath to breath, each moment flows,
In union deep, our passion grows.
Every step, a story told,
In the dance, our hearts unfold.

Moments Crafted in Kindness

A smile shared, a gentle touch,
In little things, we gain so much.
Words of comfort freely given,
In kindness, our hearts are driven.

Acts of care, like petals strewn,
In gardens where our spirits bloom.
Each moment, a treasure rare,
Crafted in love, beyond compare.

Celebrating the Ordinary

In morning light, the coffee brews,
The scent awakens slumbering hues.
A simple smile from a friend nearby,
In these small moments, joy can lie.

Children laugh as they run and play,
In their laughter, worries fade away.
A gentle breeze through the open door,
Whispers secrets of what's in store.

A book in hand, the pages turn,
In every word, the heart will yearn.
The taste of bread, warm and fresh,
In simple pleasures, we find our flesh.

Stars that twinkle in the velvet night,
A soft embrace, the world feels right.
These fleeting times, they come and go,
Yet in their warmth, our love will grow.

So here's to moments, small but grand,
The ordinary, a woven strand.
Let us celebrate with open eyes,
The beauty found in simple skies.

Heartfelt Reverberations

A whispered word, a tender touch,
The heart responds, it means so much.
In silence filled with knowing looks,
We write our verses in unseen books.

Every heartbeat shares a tale,
Emotions dancing, like a sail.
With every laugh, with every tear,
The echoes linger, ever near.

In crowded rooms, a quiet glance,
Two souls entwined in sweet romance.
The subtle pull of hands held tight,
We find our way through the dark night.

Promises made beneath the stars,
Us against the world, no bars.
In heartfelt moments, we ascend,
Each note a song, each breath a friend.

So let the rhythm guide our way,
Through trials faced, come what may.
In every heartbeat, love resounds,
A symphony of joy we've found.

The Power of Presence

In a quiet room, you sit near,
Whispers of comfort fill the air.
Time slows down, as hearts align,
In this moment, everything's fine.

Eyes meet softly, no words need said,
Emotions shared, where fears have fled.
The warmth of touch, a gentle grace,
In your presence, I find my place.

Together we laugh, together we sigh,
Building a bond that will never die.
Through storms and trials, we'll stand strong,
For in each other, we belong.

The world may shift, but we hold tight,
In every shadow, we find the light.
Our hearts entwined, a sacred trust,
In the power of presence, love is a must.

So here's to moments, both big and small,
In the dance of life, we give our all.
With you beside me, come what may,
I'll cherish each second, day by day.

Anchored in Affection

In the harbor of your embrace,
I find my solace, my safe space.
Waves may crash, storms may roar,
But anchored in love, I fear no more.

Your laughter dances on the breeze,
A melody that puts my heart at ease.
In shared glances, memories bloom,
Together we chase away the gloom.

Each whispered promise, a gentle tie,
In the fabric of us, we soar and fly.
Through trials faced, our spirits glow,
Anchored in affection, we always know.

Through life's tempests, we stand as one,
Lit by the warmth of the morning sun.
In solace found, hearts intertwine,
In love's embrace, we brightly shine.

So hold me close, through night and day,
Together we'll find our perfect way.
With every heartbeat, our love will grow,
Anchored in affection, forever we'll flow.

A Tapestry of Memories

Threads of laughter, colors bright,
We weave our stories, day and night.
Each moment captured, a vibrant hue,
In this tapestry, it's me and you.

Captured snapshots, smiles so wide,
In the fabric, love cannot hide.
Together we've stitched our hopes and dreams,
With every seam, our joy redeems.

Seasons change, yet we hold tight,
Through sunlit days and starry nights.
Woven memories, rich and deep,
In our hearts, forever they keep.

Every thread a testament, a sign,
Of the life we've built, of the love divine.
In this tapestry, we find our thread,
Interwoven moments, where we both are led.

So let's keep weaving, side by side,
In the art of me and you, we take pride.
A tapestry of memories, warm and bright,
Together we'll shine, a beautiful light.

Light in the Shadows

In the depths where shadows play,
A flicker stirs, a brand new day.
Hope ignites in the darkest night,
A tender spark, a beacon's light.

Whispers echo, fears now fade,
Illuminating paths we've laid.
In the silence, we find our voice,
A guiding star that gives us choice.

The weight of doubts may linger long,
But together we're steadfast, forever strong.
In every corner where shadows creep,
Your hand in mine, our promise we keep.

Through the maze of darkness, we will roam,
With love as our guide, we find our home.
In the tapestry of life, intertwined,
A light in the shadows is what we find.

So let the night bring its test and trial,
With you beside me, I face each mile.
In every shadow, our light will gleam,
Together we'll conquer, forever a dream.

Mirroring Emotions

In shadows cast by silvery light,
Feelings dance, in day and night.
Reflections echo, soft and clear,
Hearts entwined, we draw near.

Whispers float on gentle breeze,
Shared secrets bring warm release.
Eyes that meet, souls laid bare,
In silence found, we both dare.

Colors blend in twilight hue,
Each moment shared, a bond anew.
Laughter rings, like chimes in air,
All our truths we freely share.

Through storms we gather, firm and strong,
In every note, we find our song.
Mirroring hopes, fears, and dreams,
Together whole, or so it seems.

With shadows cast, life intertwines,
In vibrant pulse, our spirit shines.
In mirrored depths we find our way,
Emotions flow, come what may.

A Kaleidoscope of Care

In every look, a story told,
Colors shining, bright and bold.
Fragments twirl in shared delight,
Love's mosaic, pure and right.

Hands that comfort, soft embrace,
Healing warmth in every space.
Gentle smiles like morning sun,
In this dance, we are as one.

Moments shift, like turned glass,
Reflections rich, none to surpass.
Patterns change, but never fade,
Together, we are unafraid.

Through trials faced, we stand tall,
In unity, we shall not fall.
Every hue, a bond we share,
Life's a canvas, bit by bit we care.

Kaleidoscope, ever bright,
In the dark, we find our light.
Each new blend, a chance to grow,
In this love, our spirits flow.

Holding Space

In quiet moments, tensions cease,
A gentle breath brings us peace.
Here in stillness, hearts align,
In sacred trust, your pain is mine.

With open arms, I hold you tight,
In shadows deep, there waits the light.
Stories shared in whispered tones,
In this embrace, we find our home.

Every word is soft, sincere,
In this space, we shed our fear.
Vulnerability takes its stand,
Together, we both understand.

With presence pure, we mend the seams,
In each heartbeat, woven dreams.
Holding space, not just for now,
In trust's embrace, we learn just how.

Through every trial, joy and ache,
With you beside me, I won't break.
Holding space for souls that soar,
In love's embrace, we'll find our core.

Seasons of Intent

In spring's bloom, we plant the seeds,
With care and hope, we meet our needs.
Each petal bright, a dream takes flight,
In gentle winds, we chase the light.

Summer's grace, in laughter shared,
Heartbeats sync, no need for care.
Underneath the sun's warm glow,
In vibrant days, our spirits grow.

Autumn whispers, change is near,
As leaves fall, we shed our fear.
With courage born from deep within,
We dance in rhythm, let love win.

Winter calls with quiet nights,
In frosty air, we share delights.
With fires lit, our visions bright,
In sunset's glow, we see the light.

Seasons turn, a cycle true,
In every phase, I cherish you.
Intentions clear as time moves past,
In every season, love will last.

The Beauty of Unspoken Words

In silence lies a gentle grace,
A whisper dances, leaves no trace.
What's felt but never brought to light,
Holds deeper meanings, soft and bright.

A glance can speak what lips won't dare,
A bond that breathes in tender air.
Between the lines, connections grow,
In quiet hearts, the secrets flow.

Where words may falter, feelings bloom,
In hidden corners, love finds room.
The heart's own language, pure and true,
In unvoiced moments, I find you.

Beyond the sound of spoken rhyme,
The heart knows when to pause for time.
In every sigh, a truth resides,
In unspoken, our soul abides.

So let the silence paint our way,
With every heartbeat, come what may.
For in this hush, our world expands,
Holding beauty with unseen hands.

Threads of Intent

With careful hands, we weave our fate,
Each thread a promise, strong, innate.
Intentions pure, they guide our way,
In every choice, a brand new day.

A tapestry of hopes and dreams,
Together sewn, or so it seems.
Each knot a bond, each color bright,
Unfolding stories, life's delight.

The fabric holds our laughter, tears,
Threads of intent across the years.
In patterned paths, our lives entwine,
Each moment stitched, a design divine.

We'll gather strength from what we've spun,
In every task, we become one.
Through trials faced and joys embraced,
The threads of intent can't be erased.

And when we look at what we've made,
In unity, our fears do fade.
For through the loom of life, we've found,
A miracle in threads unbound.

Sculpting Shared Dreams

With hands of clay, we shape our fate,
Molding visions, never late.
Through laughter, pain, we find our form,
Sculpting dreams, we weather the storm.

Each stroke a path, each curve a sign,
In every touch, your heart meets mine.
Together we'll make the shadows dance,
In the light of our shared circumstance.

Through chisels soft, we carve our way,
A masterpiece born from night and day.
In whispered hopes, our spirits soar,
In the gallery of life, we explore.

With every dream we choose to chase,
We build a world, a sacred space.
United visions lead our stride,
In sculpting time, we walk side by side.

And when the final work is done,
We'll stand as one, beneath the sun.
For every dream we dared to chase,
Lives on in love's eternal embrace.

The Essence of Trust

In gentle hands, we place our fears,
With whispered hopes, we dry our tears.
A bond that's forged with truth and care,
In every moment, trust is rare.

Like fragile glass, we hold it tight,
In honesty, we find the light.
Through trials faced and battles won,
The essence of trust cannot be undone.

We build our walls, yet let them fall,
With opened hearts, we hear the call.
Each secret shared, it paves the way,
To trust that blossoms day by day.

In laughter's echo and silence sweet,
In shared defeat, our hearts compete.
The roots of faith grow deep and strong,
In the embrace where we both belong.

So let us dance on threads of truth,
Reviving hope, embracing youth.
In every trust, a dream takes flight,
The essence of trust shines ever bright.

The Art of Cherished Moments

In twilight's glow, we find our peace,
Each laugh a thread, we weave with ease.
A glance exchanged, the world grows small,
In silent joy, we've had it all.

With every smile, a story spun,
The fleeting times, when days are done.
Memories dance like whispers bright,
In hearts they stay, a pure delight.

The quiet hours, they hold us tight,
Soft echoes linger through the night.
Like painted skies, our moments blend,
In gentle waves that never end.

With cherished glances, hands entwined,
The beauty found, in love defined.
Beneath the stars, we softly roam,
In sacred spaces, we find home.

So hold these moments, close and dear,
In every heartbeat, feel them near.
For time will shift, but love remains,
In artful frames, through joys and pains.

Gentle Currents of Care

Like rivers flow, our kindness streams,
In tender acts, we share our dreams.
With open hearts, we find our way,
In every word, a bright array.

Through stormy seas, our sails will rise,
With gentle hands, we calm the skies.
Each gesture shared, a world reborn,
In love's embrace, we greet the dawn.

The currents guide us, side by side,
In nurturing pools, our hearts confide.
With every whisper, bonds grow strong,
In harmony, we all belong.

With caring glances, souls ignite,
In shadows deep, we find the light.
Like ripples spreading, love will grow,
In gentle currents, hearts will glow.

So let us cherish, all we share,
In every moment, show we care.
Together we'll navigate each tide,
With gentle currents, love as our guide.

Mindful Touches

With gentle grace, our fingers meet,
In soft caress, the world is sweet.
A brush of skin, electric spark,
In quiet spaces, love ignites a spark.

The warmth exchanged, a silent vow,
In every touch, the here and now.
With mindful ease, we bridge the gap,
In tender moments, life unfolds its map.

With every hug, a fortress builds,
In whispered breaths, our courage fills.
The strength in hands, a bond defined,
In mindful touches, souls aligned.

The pulse of life within our grasp,
In shared embraces, we fiercely clasp.
Let kindness flow, like rivers bend,
In mindful touches, love won't end.

So when we reach, let nothing hide,
In every moment, let love guide.
With gentle gestures, hearts will soar,
In mindful touches, we ask for more.

Heartfelt Conversations

In quiet nights, our stories flow,
With open hearts, the truth will glow.
In whispers soft, we bare our souls,
Through heartfelt talks, we become whole.

Like music played, each note sincere,
In every pause, we draw you near.
With laughter shared, we lighten loads,
In gentle words, love softly codes.

In every question, new worlds rise,
With answers found, we touch the skies.
Through every truth, our spirits dance,
In heartfelt conversations, we take the chance.

So let us speak, with love ablaze,
In fluid thoughts, we find our ways.
With open ears, we hear the call,
In heartfelt moments, we embrace it all.

In honesty, our spirits blend,
With every word, our hearts transcend.
So cherish talks, both deep and wide,
In heartfelt conversations, love will guide.

Harvesting Moments of Genuine Togetherness

In fields of laughter we meet,
Shared smiles, our hearts' steady beat.
The sun dips low, casting gold,
In these moments, our love unfolds.

We gather hopes like ripened grain,
Each memory sweet, free of pain.
Laughter lingers, tender and bright,
In the warmth of the fading light.

Hands in the earth, souls intertwined,
With each seed sown, love unconfined.
The promise of joy, in shared embrace,
Together we cherish this sacred space.

As twilight whispers, shadows play,
In this haven, where we both stay.
With every heartbeat, time stands still,
Moments of closeness, forever we fill.

So let us harvest, side by side,
In these treasures, our hearts abide.
Through every season, come what may,
Together we'll find our perfect day.

In the Silence of Thoughtful Love

In quiet corners, hearts align,
Beneath the stars, your hand in mine.
Words unspoken, warmth we share,
In the silence, love lingers there.

Gazing softly into the night,
Thoughtful glances spark the light.
No need for lines, our souls converse,
In this stillness, we gently immerse.

Moments stretch like shadows cast,
In tender silence, we hold fast.
Time dissolves, as breaths collide,
In calm reflection, love is our guide.

Every heartbeat, a silent song,
With you, my dear, I know I belong.
In thoughtfulness, our spirits soar,
In this silence, we find much more.

So let the world fade far away,
In this stillness, together we'll stay.
With every heartbeat, love grows deep,
In moments of silence, shared secrets we keep.

Heartstrings in Harmony

Two melodies blend as we play,
In perfect rhythm, come what may.
Your laughter dances through the air,
In each note, there's love laid bare.

With strings entwined, our hearts express,
A symphony, life's sweet caress.
In harmony, we find our tune,
As the stars beneath us commune.

Every hummed verse is a memory,
Crafted in love's sweet mystery.
Weaving our hopes through strum and beat,
In every chord, our lives complete.

So let this song echo through years,
In joy and laughter, through all tears.
With each heartstring that we entwine,
Together we'll make this harmony shine.

As the final note lingers sweet,
In this melody, we find our beat.
Together, forever, side by side,
With heartstrings in harmony, love our guide.

Intentional Embrace

In each embrace, a story's told,
Of warmth and safety, love so bold.
Intentional, our hearts entwine,
In every hug, you're truly mine.

With open arms, I hold you near,
In silent comfort, we overcome fear.
Each gentle squeeze speaks what words can't,
In this connection, our souls chant.

Every meeting, a cherished gift,
Through storms of life, our spirits lift.
In these moments, we choose to stay,
Intentional love lights the way.

As time unfolds, our bond will grow,
In every hug, our love will flow.
With gentle whispers, through night and day,
In intentional embrace, come what may.

So let us dance in this timeless space,
Finding joy, our safe, sacred place.
Together we flourish, side by side,
In the power of love, our hearts abide.

Heartbeats in the Quiet

In the stillness, whispers play,
Softly wrapping night in gray.
Every heartbeat, a gentle song,
In this silence, we belong.

Stars peer down, a watchful gaze,
Filling darkness with their blaze.
Moments freeze like falling snow,
In the quiet, love will grow.

Moonlight drapes a silver thread,
In this hush, our fears are shed.
Captured dreams in starlit beams,
In the silence, we find dreams.

Time suspends with breathless grace,
In the dark, we find our place.
Together woven, souls entwined,
In the quiet, peace we find.

Softly now, the shadows blend,
As the night begins to mend.
With each heartbeat, I feel you near,
In this moment, crystal clear.

Mapping Our Togetherness

Across the miles, our paths align,
In every heartbeat, yours and mine.
We chart a course through storms and calm,
In our togetherness, a balm.

Every step, a shared embrace,
In fleeting moments, time we trace.
Your laughter echoes in my mind,
In this journey, love defined.

Through winding roads, our story flows,
With whispered hopes that gently grows.
Hand in hand, we carve new ways,
In our togetherness, endless days.

Like stars that sparkle in the night,
Guiding each other toward the light.
With every turn, our spirits soar,
In this map, there's always more.

At every crossroad, you and I,
Navigating as we rise high.
Together, we're a tapestry,
In our togetherness, we're free.

Dialogues of the Heart

In quiet moments, we exchange,
A language soft, yet never strange.
Words unspoken, feelings shared,
Dialogues of love, deeply cared.

In every glance, a story told,
In every smile, a warmth unfolds.
Listening closely, hearts will speak,
In this language, we're not weak.

Through tangled thoughts and dreams so bright,
We find our way in darkest night.
Echoed sighs and tender tones,
In this dance, we're not alone.

Trust is woven through our chats,
In laughter's shade, where kindness sits.
Every heartbeat, a rhythm's art,
In this dialogue, two become smart.

As time flows on, our bond will grow,
In every response, love will flow.
With every moment, hearts relay,
In dialogues of love, we'll stay.

A Promise of Patience

In the waiting, seeds are sown,
Gentle whispers softly known.
Time will shape our hearts anew,
In this promise, I choose you.

Through changing tides, we will stand,
Facing storms, we'll hold the hand.
With unwavering faith, we'll rise,
In this moment, love's sunrise.

Days may stretch and shadows cast,
Yet in patience, love holds fast.
Step by step, we'll find our way,
In this promise, come what may.

Every heartbeat whispers slow,
Trusting in the love we grow.
In every pause, our spirits dance,
In this promise, there's a chance.

Tenderly, we'll share our dreams,
Mending seams with golden beams.
With patient hearts, we'll learn to sway,
In this promise, love will stay.

Hearts in Harmony

In quiet moments, we align,
Two souls entwined, a sacred sign.
With gentle whispers, our dreams flow,
Together we bloom, love's radiant glow.

Through storms and sun, we stand as one,
In laughter's echo, our journey's begun.
In every heartbeat, a melody plays,
A symphony of love that never decays.

Fingers entwined, we dance through night,
In the soft embrace of luminous light.
With every step, our spirits glide,
In this shared rhythm, hope and pride.

Paths interwoven, fate's sweet thread,
In silence shared, no words need be said.
As time flows by, our passion stays,
In the warmth of your gaze, my heart sways.

Embracing the stillness, we melt away,
In deep devotion, come what may.
For in your heart, I've found my home,
Together forever, no need to roam.

Kisses Beyond the Clock

In stolen moments, time stands still,
A tender kiss, a heart to fill.
With every touch, the world fades out,
In your arms, I know no doubt.

As midnight whispers sweet and low,
Beneath the stars, our passions grow.
Each stolen glance, a spark ignites,
Kisses beyond clocks, endless nights.

In lingering warmth, our spirits soar,
A timeless dance on love's grand floor.
With every heartbeat, we intertwine,
In a sacred space, so divine.

The world may rush, yet we find pause,
In soft caresses, our hearts' applause.
Through moonlit dreams, we drift as one,
In this embrace, our fears are undone.

For as the hourglass slowly spills,
Each precious kiss, a world it fills.
In love's embrace, we find our clock,
A dance that sways, with every tick tock.

The Art of Thoughtful Embrace

In the quiet glow of evening's grace,
We find the art in a warm embrace.
With gentle fingers, our souls align,
In a world of chaos, your heart is mine.

Every heartbeat tells a story sweet,
In tender moments where silence meets.
With every sigh, a canvas we paint,
Love's masterpiece, never faint.

We share our dreams in whispers low,
In thoughtful gazes, our feelings show.
Through every challenge, together we grow,
In the art of love, our colors flow.

With open hearts, we break the mold,
In every whisper, our secrets told.
Bound by trust, our spirits entwine,
In this embrace, everything's fine.

As we navigate this dance of fate,
The art of love, we cultivate.
With every touch, serenity reigns,
In a world of stillness, love remains.

Whispers of Purposeful Affection

In softest tones, love's whispers glow,
A language spoken, hearts in tow.
With every glance, a meaning deep,
In purposeful paths, our promises keep.

Through gentle winds, our voices rise,
In every heartbeat, no need for lies.
With every touch, intentions clear,
In this dance, we conquer fear.

As sunlight dances on morning dew,
In whispered dreams, I find you true.
Our laughter fills the air with cheer,
In purposeful affection, we draw near.

With every movement, a shared embrace,
In fleeting moments, we find our place.
With written notes on love's soft page,
In whispers shared, we turn the page.

Together we weave a tapestry bright,
In every whisper, love takes flight.
With open hearts, we chart our way,
In purposeful affection, come what may.

Moments That Matter

In a quiet place we stand,
Time stands still, a soft command.
Silent hearts begin to speak,
In gentle words, we find the peak.

Eyes that sparkle, stories shared,
In every glance, a truth laid bare.
Holding tight to fleeting days,
Finding joy in simple ways.

Echoes of laughter fill the air,
Memories woven with love and care.
These moments tied with golden thread,
In our hearts, they bloom instead.

A whisper through the autumn leaves,
Each shared smile, a hope that breathes.
Together we'll chase the sunset's glow,
And treasure each moment as it flows.

As time slips quietly like sand,
We will walk this path, hand in hand.
For every heartbeat sings a tune,
Of moments precious as the moon.

Fostering Kindness

In the warmth of a shared embrace,
Kindness blooms, a gentle grace.
Small gestures brightening the day,
In simple ways, we find our way.

A smile exchanged on bustling streets,
A helping hand, where kindness meets.
Lifting others, we rise above,
Creating ripples with our love.

Words of comfort, soft and sweet,
In every heart, a rhythmic beat.
Fostering compassion in the rain,
We're all connected through joy and pain.

Together we can change the tide,
With open hearts, let love abide.
In every soul, a light we find,
Fostering kindness, forever intertwined.

So let the spirit of kindness flow,
In every corner, let it grow.
A world united, hand in hand,
With kindness spreading through the land.

Seeds of Understanding

In every thought, a seed is sown,
In silent spaces, truths are grown.
Listen closely to the breeze,
Understanding flows with ease.

Between the whispers and the shouts,
Empathy shines through all doubts.
Digging deeper, we unravel,
With each step, new paths we travel.

Cultivating trust, we find our way,
Through every night into the day.
With open hearts, we take a stand,
Together we can understand.

Planting dreams where gardens bloom,
In every heart, a shared room.
Nurturing bonds, we grow as one,
Seeds of understanding shine like the sun.

So let us tend this sacred ground,
Where compassion's roots are found.
With every moment joy extends,
In the garden of our friends.

Hands That Hold

With hands that hold, we stand so strong,
Through trials deep and nights so long.
In every clasp, a promise made,
A union forged, never to fade.

In laughter shared and tears we weep,
These tender bonds our hearts shall keep.
With every touch, we light the way,
Together braving night and day.

Building dreams with every thread,
As journeys start and stories spread.
In gentle strength, we find our place,
In hands that hold, we feel the grace.

A safe embrace in storms that rage,
With every heartbeat, we turn the page.
Through the years, through thin and thick,
Our hands entwined, a magic trick.

So here's to love that never parts,
In every hand, a thousand hearts.
Together we'll weather all of life,
These hands that hold cut through the strife.

The Canvas of Us

On the canvas our colors blend,
Brush strokes that never end.
Each hue tells a story bright,
Together we create our light.

In moments shared, we find the way,
A masterpiece that won't decay.
Every line, a whispered thought,
In this artwork, we are caught.

The shadows speak of trials faced,
Yet in the shadows, joy's embraced.
Through every shade, we learn to grow,
Together, always, as we flow.

With each splash, our hearts align,
In sync like rhythm, pure and fine.
This canvas stretches wide and far,
Reflecting who we really are.

In vibrant dreams, we'll find our way,
Through every night, through every day.
The canvas of us, forever true,
A living art, just me and you.

Purposeful Passions

In the fire of dreams, we ignite,
Passions that soar, taking flight.
Chasing the echoes of our calls,
Determined souls that never falls.

With every step, we plant our seeds,
Nurturing hopes, fulfilling needs.
Through trials faced, we persevere,
As purpose guides us, year by year.

Crafting our paths with loving care,
In the light of hopes, we dare.
Each heartbeat sings a vibrant song,
Together, we are brave and strong.

In unity, our strength revealed,
With passion's fire, we are healed.
Purposeful journeys hand in hand,
In this vast, extraordinary land.

Our passions blaze, forever bright,
Turning the dark into pure light.
With every heartbeat, we embrace,
Purposeful passions, our sacred space.

Navigating Through Trust

In the waters, calm and deep,
We navigate, our bonds to keep.
Trust the anchor, strong and true,
Guiding us with every hue.

With charts of dreams, we sail along,
Together, where hearts belong.
Through storms that may cloud the way,
Trust will guide us, come what may.

Each wave whispers secrets shared,
In the depths, love is declared.
Hand in hand, we'll face the tide,
In this journey, side by side.

Navigating through the trials near,
With every choice, we draw you near.
In trust we find a sacred ground,
Where joy and peace are always found.

As the stars light up our path,
We stand united, face the wrath.
Through every journey, far and wide,
Navigating trust as our guide.

Echoes of Togetherness

In the whispers of the night,
Echoes linger, soft and light.
Together, hearts beat as one,
In the light of the setting sun.

Each moment shared, a treasured tune,
Dancing lightly beneath the moon.
In laughter's joy and sorrow's tears,
Together we conquer all our fears.

Through the echoes, our voices blend,
Writing stories that never end.
In the silence, love finds a way,
Guiding us through every day.

In harmony, we rise and fall,
Answering life's resounding call.
Each memory, a gentle thread,
Weaving paths where hearts have led.

With every heartbeat, we find grace,
Echoes of us in time and space.
Together we stand, forever strong,
In the symphony of our song.

Stargazing Beyond the Clouds of Routine

In the silence of night, we rise,
Eyes cast upward, dreams in disguise.
Stars whisper tales of journeys far,
Beyond the veil of the morning star.

Each twinkle a wish that softly glows,
Guiding us where the wild wind blows.
Routine fades under the cosmic light,
As we dance with shadows, lost from sight.

Cycles break, and time stands still,
Hearts open wide, eager to feel.
Above the clouds, we find our grace,
In the vastness of this timeless space.

Let go of the pull of gravity's might,
Embrace the wonder of the infinite night.
For in the cosmos, we find our place,
Stargazing beyond the mundane chase.

With every glance, new worlds awake,
Awash in light, our spirits take.
Journey onward, hand in hand,
Catching stardust upon this land.

The Poetry of Considerate Hearts

In the gentle hush of a caring glance,
Words fade softly, lost in a dance.
Every heartbeat, a verse so sweet,
Bound by kindness, where souls meet.

Thoughtful gestures weave a thread,
Through the tapestry of what we said.
Knowing the weight that silence can bear,
We offer warmth, a love laid bare.

Amidst the noise of the hurried throng,
Our hearts compose a tender song.
With understanding as our guiding light,
We forge connections that feel just right.

A smile shared, a hand to hold,
The poetry of kindness, a language bold.
In small moments, true beauty lies,
In considerate hearts, the deepest ties.

Together we write in the margins of time,
With hearts that beat in perfect rhyme.
For every act of love, a line,
In the poem of lives, beautifully entwined.

Kindling the Fire of Intentional Souls

In the stillness, we gather round,
Intentions whispered, a sacred sound.
Fires ignite with the power of dreams,
Where passion flows in radiant streams.

Each ember sparks a vivid glow,
Fueling desires that softly sow.
With every breath, we tend the flame,
Lighting the darkness, calling our name.

Awake and alive with purpose clear,
Hearts aligned, no room for fear.
In every heartbeat, a choice to make,
To light the path for each other's sake.

Together we build, with hands held tight,
Nurturing hope in the deep of night.
For intentional souls blaze brightly,
In the warmth of connection, we grow lightly.

So let us stoke this fervent fire,
With dreams and wishes that never tire.
In the dance of hearts, we find our role,
Kindling the fire of intentional souls.

A Tapestry of Shared Dreams

Like threads that weave in the quiet light,
We share our dreams, lifting them high.
Colors blend in a vibrant stream,
Creating a tapestry of what we deem.

Each story told, a knot of trust,
Binding us close in the warmth of us.
With every laugh, we intertwine,
Our hopes and wishes seamlessly align.

In this fabric of life, joys and scars,
Are stitched together like guiding stars.
Hand in hand, our visions unite,
A symphony of dreams in the night.

Through storms and calm, we stand as one,
In the brilliance of rays from the setting sun.
For every dream shared, another thread,
In the tapestry where love is fed.

So let us cherish this work of art,
A patchwork of souls, each playing a part.
In the intricate weave, we find our way,
A tapestry of shared dreams every day.

Ties That Bind with Purpose

In shadows cast by dreams so bright,
We weave our stories, hearts take flight.
With every glance, a silent vow,
Together strong, we flourish now.

Through trials faced, we stand as one,
In laughter shared, our journeys spun.
With open arms and eyes so clear,
Our purpose found, we hold it dear.

In whispers soft, we share our fate,
Embracing love, we celebrate.
Through storms and calm, our spirits rise,
The ties that bind, the heart replies.

With every challenge, hand in hand,
A stronger force, we understand.
Together built on trust and grace,
In unity, we find our place.

As seasons change, we learn and grow,
With every breath, our love will show.
In this domain where souls entwine,
We cherish all, the ties that bind.

The Canvas of Meaningful Moments

Each stroke of time paints vivid hues,
In every breath, a tale we choose.
With colors bright, our laughter sings,
On life's canvas, joy it brings.

Moments cherished, soft and rare,
In quiet corners, love laid bare.
With gentle hands, we craft the day,
In every heartbeat, dreams at play.

Through frames of gold, our story glows,
In faded ink, the memory flows.
With family close, and friends so dear,
We gather round, our hearts sincere.

Beneath the stars, we share our fears,
In honest words, we dry our tears.
Together strong, we face the night,
On this canvas, we find our light.

Every brushstroke whispers low,
In lasting images, love will grow.
A tapestry of moments bright,
On this canvas, our souls take flight.

Aligning Souls with Awareness

In quiet spaces, thoughts align,
With open hearts, our spirits shine.
Through mindful steps, we find our way,
In every moment, here to stay.

Each glance exchanged, a knowing glance,
In every heartbeat, a sacred dance.
With presence felt, we breathe as one,
Awareness blossoms, battles won.

Through chaos faced, we find the calm,
In gentle words, we share the balm.
With kindness sown, the seeds we plant,
Aligning souls, our spirits chant.

Through trials deep and storms that rage,
We turn the page, we set the stage.
With every laugh and tear we share,
We bring to life the love we bear.

In unity, our vision clear,
With every moment, love draws near.
As souls align with pure intent,
In shared awareness, we are meant.

Meditations on Cherished Bonds

In quiet moments, we reflect,
On treasured ties, our hearts connect.
With whispered thoughts of love professed,
In gentle peace, our souls find rest.

Through memories shared, so softly bound,
In laughter's echo, joy is found.
With hands entwined, we feel the glow,
Through every storm, our love will flow.

In timeless grace, we dance our dance,
With every glance, we find our chance.
With gratitude, we hold each dear,
In cherished bonds, we conquer fear.

Through trials faced and obstacles met,
In the warmth of love, we won't forget.
With every heartbeat, trust we weave,
In meditation, we believe.

As twilight fades and dreams unfold,
In gentle whispers, stories told.
In bonds of love, we shall remain,
Together strong, through joy and pain.

Embracing Each Imperfection

In the cracks of our being, we find light,
Every flaw, a story, shining bright.
Embrace the shadows, let them be,
For in each blemish, we are free.

The scars that we carry, rough yet true,
Are testaments of battles we've been through.
A tapestry woven with threads of gold,
In accepting our wounds, we are bold.

With every stumble, we learn the dance,
Life's not perfect; it's a chance.
To gather the pieces, to make them whole,
In the art of living, we find our soul.

Each imperfection, a brushstroke fine,
Crafting a portrait, uniquely divine.
Accept the chaos, the joy, the pain,
In the storm of life, we grow and gain.

So here we stand, flaws on display,
In the beauty of life, we choose to stay.
Embracing each moment, both dark and light,
In imperfection, we take flight.

Anchors and Wings

In the depths of the sea, silence waits,
Anchors hold tight, while freedom abates.
Yet above the waves, the sky does call,
Wings stretched wide, we rise and fall.

Roots run deep in familiar ground,
Anchors supporting us, safe and sound.
But the wind whispers soft, a promise of flight,
Wings that beckon to soar out of sight.

Each choice we make, a tether or rise,
Anchors keep us, while wings touch the skies.
In the dance of the heart, we find our way,
Navigating life, come what may.

Both anchors and wings, a delicate thread,
Balancing dreams and the path we tread.
In the journey of life, we learn to blend,
Finding strength in both, till the very end.

So let us embrace, the pull and the push,
In the calm of the sea, in the wild, we rush.
With anchors to ground us, and wings to inspire,
We'll sail through the storm, igniting our fire.

Paintbrushes of the Heart

With colors vibrant, emotions flow,
Each stroke a feeling, a heart's inner glow.
The canvas of life, both vast and wide,
Paintbrushes ready, with love as our guide.

Joy splashes bright in shades of gold,
While echoes of sorrow, a story untold.
Mixing the hues, we find our truth,
In the art of living, we reclaim our youth.

With every heartbeat, the brush moves swift,
Creating a masterpiece, a divine gift.
Imperfectly perfect, we dance with fate,
In the gallery of dreams, we celebrate.

Through valleys of shadows, we find our light,
Painting perceptions, wrongs into right.
Each moment a canvas, each choice a hue,
With paintbrushes of the heart, we renew.

So let us create, with passion and grace,
In every layer, life's honest embrace.
With colors unfurling, our spirits embark,
Crafting the beauty, igniting the spark.

The Journey Within

In silence we wander, the mind's vast maze,
Seeking the truth, through life's winding ways.
Each thought a step, each breath a sign,
On the journey within, we intertwine.

The echoes of whispers, the past lingers near,
Memories flicker, as dreams persevere.
With courage we delve, into depths unknown,
In the heart's sacred chamber, we find our own.

Mountains of doubt and rivers of grace,
Navigating shadows, we quicken our pace.
A quest for the self, beneath layers of guise,
Revealing the essence, the soul's true rise.

Through valleys of turmoil, we learn to embrace,
The journey is long, but we quicken our pace.
With each revelation that lights up the dark,
We gather the wisdom, igniting the spark.

So here in the stillness, we tenderly tread,
With open hearts guiding, where the spirit is led.
In the mosaic of life, we stitch every seam,
The journey within, our everlasting dream.

The Dance of Sincerity

In shadows cast by truth's warm light,
We sway between the day and night.
With honesty, our movements blend,
In every step, a heart to mend.

A rhythm slow, yet ever bold,
A story whispered, yet retold.
In trust, we find a space to share,
A binding force, a gentle care.

Each glance a promise, each touch a spark,
In the silence, love leaves its mark.
Together, we twirl, we spin and glide,
In this dance, we do not hide.

Our laughter echoes, crisp and clear,
In every moment, we draw near.
With open hearts, we take our chance,
Creating worlds within this dance.

As music fades into the night,
We hold each other, feeling right.
In sincerity, we find our way,
A dance of truths that never sway.

Bonds We Weave

In threads of kindness, strong and bright,
We stitch together day and night.
Each word a fiber, soft yet sure,
In unity, we find our cure.

Through trials faced and joys embraced,
In each connection, time is graced.
A tapestry of lives combined,
In every heart, love intertwined.

With laughter shared and burdens cast,
We find a shelter, built to last.
Through storms of life, we stand as one,
In bonds we've forged, our battles won.

In quiet moments, echoes ring,
The weight of love, a treasured thing.
With open arms, we welcome strife,
In every bond, we find our life.

As seasons change and years unfold,
The stories shared become pure gold.
In every thread, a tale we weave,
Together as we learn to believe.

The Language of Awareness

In moments still, the whispers grow,
A silent place where thoughts can flow.
With open eyes, we start to see,
The world around, in harmony.

Each breath a word, each pause a sigh,
In presence felt, we learn to fly.
The rhythm of life, in sync we stand,
With heart and mind, we join the band.

With gentle steps, we tread the ground,
In mindfulness, the truth is found.
As colors shift and shadows play,
In nature's dance, we find our way.

Awareness blooms, a flower bright,
In every moment, pure delight.
To listen close, to feel the air,
In stillness, we become aware.

In shared experiences, we grow wise,
The language spoken through our eyes.
In every heartbeat, life's refrain,
An eternal lesson learned again.

Nurtured through Stillness

In quietude, the spirit thrives,
In gentle calm, our essence lives.
A refuge found from worldly noise,
In stillness, we reclaim our joys.

With every sigh, the heart expands,
In soft embrace, the soul withstands.
Through moments still, awareness blooms,
In silence, light dispels the gloom.

The whispers of the mind are hushed,
In tranquil waves, our worries crushed.
A sanctuary in each breath,
Through stillness, we confront our depth.

With nature's pulse as our guide,
In peaceful grounds, we abide.
In petals' fall and rising tides,
Through stillness, our wisdom strides.

As time unfolds, we find our grace,
In muted spaces, we embrace.
In every pause, life's essence reveals,
In stillness, love is what it heals.

Connections Woven with Heartstrings

In the quiet night, we share our dreams,
Gentle whispers flow like soft moonbeams.
Each laughter binds us, a tapestry tight,
Woven in love, glowing through the night.

Through trials faced, our strength unfolds,
In every challenge, our bond molds.
Hand in hand, we walk this lane,
Connections forged, through joy and pain.

Every memory, a thread in the weave,
In the heart's fabric, we firmly believe.
With every touch, with every sigh,
The heartstrings connect, as days slip by.

In the warmth of hugs, a promise kept,
With every heartbeat, our secrets are swept.
In the cadence of life, we dance so free,
Together we are, just you and me.

As time moves on, old ages may part,
But the connections linger in every heart.
For love is the thread that time cannot sever,
In the tapestry of life, we are forever.

The Palette of Heartfelt Intent

Brush strokes of kindness, colors that bloom,
With every gesture, we banish the gloom.
A splash of laughter, hues rich and bright,
Painting the canvas in soft morning light.

From shades of blue for the moments of pain,
To vibrant reds where the passions sustain.
Each color a story, our hearts intertwine,
In the palette of love, where emotions align.

With gentle pastels of sincere embrace,
We create our own world, a nurturing place.
In every stroke, we find peace and delight,
Crafting our future, igniting the night.

The whispers of green in the leaves of our dreams,
Flow through us gently, like flowing streams.
In the masterpiece drawn from every intent,
The world finds its beauty; our hearts are content.

So let us paint boldly, with brushes of fate,
In this vibrant mural, let's celebrate.
For the palette of life, so vivid and true,
Is colored with love, and painted by you.

Unwritten Letters of Affection

In the still of the night, thoughts take flight,
Words held in silence, cloaked from the light.
With every breath, my heart starts to pen,
Unwritten letters, longing for when.

The ink of my hope bleeds through the pages,
In dreams and wishes, love never ages.
Each unsent note carries secrets untold,
Wrapped in the warmth, like a blanket of gold.

Through every heartbeat, a story unfolds,
In quiet moments, affection beholds.
With the thrill of a word lost in the air,
Unwritten letters, a bond we both share.

Perhaps someday, in the glow of dawn,
These whispered feelings will no longer be drawn.
For in each letter lies the tender truth,
Of love and affection, eternal in youth.

So I dream of the day when words find their way,
On these unwritten pages, in soft hearts they play.
Every letter, a promise, forever to keep,
In the silence of longing, our love runs deep.

Radiance in Every Thoughtful Glance

In the flutter of eyes, the world ignites,
Silent conversations, pure as the nights.
With every glance, stories awaken,
Radiance beams, no heart left forsaken.

Through the depths of gazes, emotions lie,
In the dance of the mind, where secrets slip by.
Each shared look, a universe spun,
Reflecting the love that can't be undone.

The warmth of warmth, in a fleeting stare,
Moments are captured, delicate and rare.
Fragments of truth in the corners of sight,
Radiance shines, like stars in the night.

In the art of connection, our souls intertwine,
With every glance, we taste the divine.
Unspoken feelings, we carefully weave,
In the artful embrace, we begin to believe.

So let us cherish these moments, my dear,
For the beauty of glances forever draws near.
In the radiance shared, we eternally dance,
Lost in the magic of every chance glance.

Embracing the Everyday

In morning light, we rise anew,
With coffee warm, and skies so blue.
The whispers of the day unfold,
In simple joys, our stories told.

A gentle breeze through open doors,
Brings laughter in from nature's shores.
Each moment shared, a treasure bright,
In the embrace of morning light.

The mundane tasks we often face,
Transform in love's warm, sweet embrace.
From dishes piled to floors that gleam,
Each duty sings a hidden dream.

At twilight's glow, we gather near,
With shared reflections, hearts sincere.
The everyday, a canvas bare,
Painted with love, beyond compare.

So let us dance in life's ballet,
And find the magic in each day.
For in the small, the big unfolds,
Embracing life, our hearts behold.

Echoes of an Intentional Soul

In quiet moments, whispers grow,
Echoes of paths we choose to sow.
Intentions cast like seeds in spring,
From mindful thoughts, our spirits sing.

Each breath a chance to start anew,
To chase the light, and find the true.
With every step, our vision clear,
An intentional life, free from fear.

The world unfolds in tender grace,
As we discover our own pace.
With love as guide, we gently tread,
Creating futures, not just threads.

Moments captured, hearts aligned,
Each choice a thread that we unwind.
Echoes linger, soft and wise,
In the simplest, sincere ties.

So let us walk this path as one,
With open hearts 'til day is done.
An intentional soul finds its way,
In every dawn, in every sway.

The Craft of Listening

In silence shared, we find our voice,
The craft of listening, a choice.
With open ears and hearts awake,
We weave connections, give and take.

A gentle nod, a knowing glance,
Each story told, a sacred dance.
With empathy, we find our ground,
In each other's truths, we're bound.

To hear the whispers in the rain,
The subtle joys, the tender pain.
With patience, we embrace the space,
As words descend, they find their place.

In every pause, there's room to grow,
The craft of listening starts to flow.
With kindness woven through each word,
A tapestry of souls inferred.

So let us cultivate this art,
To truly listen, to take part.
For every heart has tales to share,
In the craft of listening, we care.

Heartbeats in Sync

Two souls entwined, a rhythm found,
In every heartbeat, love unbound.
With every glance, a pulse ignites,
Together weaving days and nights.

With laughter clear, and tears set free,
Our heartbeats dance like waves at sea.
In sync they play, a symphony,
The song of you, the song of me.

Through trials faced and mountains climbed,
Our heartbeats echo, intertwined.
In moments shared, both calm and wild,
We are together, heart and child.

With each embrace, we find our way,
Through storms that fade and skies turned gray.
In harmony, we rise and fall,
A love that answers every call.

So let us cherish every beat,
In paths we walk and dreams we meet.
For heartbeats in sync, a timeless song,
Together we are, where we belong.

The Grace of Touch

In whispers soft and sweet,
Our fingers brush, a fleeting heat.
A moment shared, hearts intertwine,
In gentle warmth, your hand in mine.

From daybreak light to twilight glow,
The grace of touch in ebb and flow.
A silent pact, a bond so true,
In every glance, I find you too.

Through storms we stand, united strong,
In every trial, we belong.
With every hug, a promise made,
In love's embrace, we'll never fade.

And as the world around us spins,
With every touch, a new day begins.
In quiet moments, our hearts align,
In the grace of touch, pure love we find.

Together we craft memories bright,
In every hold, there's pure delight.
With fingers laced and spirits high,
The grace of touch will never die.

Capturing Fleeting Time

Time dances lightly, a fleeting wisp,
In every heartbeat, a gentle lisp.
Moments gather, like grains of sand,
In the hourglass of life, we stand.

A snapshot caught, a memory frozen,
In laughter's echo, love's sweet token.
With every glance, we etch our tale,
Against the winds that twist and sail.

A fleeting whisper, it slips away,
Yet in our hearts, it loves to stay.
In joys and sorrows, we weave and bind,
Capturing time, a treasure to find.

Seasons change, yet we remain,
In the dance of time, hearts entertain.
With every moment, a piece of grace,
In capturing time, we find our place.

So hold me tight as moments flee,
In each embrace, eternity.
Let us savor the fleeting light,
Capturing time, our hearts take flight.

Resonance of Souls

Deep within, our spirits gleam,
In quiet nights, we share a dream.
A melody played on heartstrings fine,
In the resonance, our souls align.

An echo calls from far and near,
In every laugh, in every tear.
In harmony, we rise and fall,
The resonance sings, a sacred call.

Through every storm and sunlit day,
With every word, we find our way.
In whispered secrets, our vows unfolds,
In the resonance, love's story told.

Connected threads, our lives entwined,
In life's vast dance, two hearts combined.
In cosmic rhythms, we find our role,
In the resonance, the merging soul.

So let us walk this path of light,
In unity, we take our flight.
For in each heartbeat's gentle toll,
We find the resonance of our souls.

The Garden of Us

In a garden where hearts bloom bright,
Love's petals open, kissed by light.
Rooted deep in rich, warm soil,
In the garden of us, we tirelessly toil.

With each new dawn, our hopes arise,
In laughter's chorus, beneath blue skies.
Tender hands nurture dreams so sweet,
In the garden of us, life feels complete.

Blooming flowers, vibrant and bold,
In colors painted, our story told.
Through seasons' change, we grow and thrive,
In the garden of us, love is alive.

Amidst the thorns, we find our way,
In every challenge, love will stay.
With every sigh and gentle kiss,
In the garden of us, we find our bliss.

So let us wander through this place,
Each petal kissed with love's embrace.
In every moment, come what may,
In the garden of us, forever stay.

Echoing Kindness

In whispers soft, we share our grace,
A gentle touch in this vast space.
Hearts open wide, we dare to feel,
Kindness blooms, a wondrous meal.

Through every shadow, light will creep,
Promises made, our souls to keep.
With every smile, we paint the day,
Echoes of hope, forever stay.

In laughter shared, we find our song,
A dance of hearts, where we belong.
With every word, we build a bridge,
Connecting paths, no need to hedge.

Each small act, a ripple's flow,
Kindness sown, it starts to grow.
Across the world, our love will soar,
Echoing back, forevermore.

As stars align in the dark night,
Kindness shines, a guiding light.
Together, we weave this tapestry,
Of echoing love, eternally.

A Harmonious Palette

With strokes of sunlight, colors blend,
Creating dreams that never end.
Nature's canvas, vast and bright,
A harmonious dance, pure delight.

From emerald greens to cerulean skies,
In every hue, a memory lies.
We gather shades, diverse and rare,
In unity, we paint the air.

Each sunset whispers tales untold,
Of vibrant moments, brave and bold.
The brush we wield, a heart's embrace,
In every stroke, a sacred space.

The rhythms of the world resound,
In every color, love is found.
Together we create, ignite,
A palette rich, a shared delight.

In every heartbeat, colors play,
A symphony of night and day.
In harmony, our spirits rise,
A masterpiece beneath the skies.

The Gift of Attention

A whispered breath, a gentle look,
The power found in every nook.
In silence held, connections grow,
The gift of attention starts to flow.

In crowded rooms, we find the space,
To truly see, to seek their face.
In every pause, a world unveiled,
With open hearts, our fears curtailed.

The stories shared in fleeting time,
Moments cherished, pure and sublime.
With every smile, we make a vow,
To honor here, to live the now.

With focused eyes, we breathe them in,
An understanding where love begins.
In every gaze, a bond so strong,
The gift of attention makes us belong.

Together, we nurture, we allow,
With tender hearts, we take a bow.
In this present, let kindness reign,
The gift of attention, our shared gain.

Weaving Moments of Joy

In threads of laughter, smiles are spun,
Each moment cherished, everyone.
With every heartbeat, stories grow,
Weaving moments, lighting the flow.

In gentle whispers, secrets share,
The fabric strong, enriched with care.
Through seasons changing, colors fade,
But joy remains, a bond we've made.

With every hug and hand we hold,
A tapestry of lives unfolds.
We find our strength in unity,
Weaving together, you and me.

As threads entwine amidst the night,
We craft a quilt, our hearts alight.
In every stitch, a love precise,
Moments of joy, a true paradise.

So let us dance in colors bright,
A woven tale, pure and light.
In joyous rhythm, we will flow,
Creating magic, weaving joy.

The Chorus of Mindful Hearts

In the stillness, whispers play,
Echoes of thoughts in bright array.
Hearts align in harmony,
A gentle song, our symphony.

Breathing deep, we find our ground,
In every silence, peace is found.
Each heartbeat sings, a truth so clear,
United souls, we gather near.

With every glance, a story told,
In every touch, a warmth of gold.
Mindful paths where kindness flows,
In the garden, love still grows.

Moments woven, threads of grace,
Every face a sacred space.
We lift each other, hand in hand,
In this chorus, we all stand.

Gentle spirits, open wide,
In this trust, we safely bide.
Through trials faced, we learn to dance,
In the rhythm, we find our chance.

Painting Dreams with Gentle Hands

Colors splash on canvases bright,
With every stroke, we bring to light.
Dreams unfurl in soft embrace,
In our hearts, a sacred space.

Brushes dance like whispers soft,
Creating worlds where spirits loft.
Imagination takes its flight,
In this realm of pure delight.

Each hue a story, each line a song,
In this journey, we belong.
Through the chaos, beauty streams,
We are the keepers of our dreams.

With gentle hands, we shape the fate,
In every moment, love creates.
Masterpieces born from the soul,
In every flick, we feel whole.

Together, let our spirits blend,
As we create, begin, and mend.
In every canvas, a life we share,
In the art of love, we find our care.

A Symphony of Aware Emotions

Feelings deep, a vibrant score,
In every heartbeat, we explore.
Strings of joy and notes of pain,
In the melody, we are lain.

Through the silence, crescendos rise,
Voices weave through lows and highs.
With awareness, we embrace,
Every sound, a tender grace.

Harmony in each breath we take,
Each emotion, a path we make.
In the shadows, light shines through,
In this symphony, we renew.

Together, we create the tune,
Lifting spirits, like a balloon.
In this concert of the heart,
We find connection, play our part.

Listen close to the song within,
In this rhythm, let love begin.
A dance of feelings, rich and bold,
In this symphony, our souls unfold.

Sowing Seeds of Deliberate Joy

In the garden, hearts align,
Planting seeds in moments fine.
With each action, joy will grow,
In gratitude, we sow and sow.

Tending blooms with mindful care,
Watered thoughts, a love we share.
In the sunlight, laughter shines,
Nurtured joy through endless times.

Roots of kindness intertwine,
In this soil, our souls design.
Through storms of life, we stand so tall,
In every struggle, we find our call.

Harvesting the fruits we've grown,
In this journey, we are never alone.
Every smile, a seed we've sown,
In this bond, our hearts have flown.

Delight in moments, savor each,
In this garden, love we teach.
With open hearts, we plant our joy,
Embracing life, nothing can destroy.

Illuminating Paths of Heartfelt Care

In shadows deep where kindness blooms,
The gentle light dispels the glooms.
With open arms, we share our ways,
Creating warmth in lonely days.

A whispered word, a tender glance,
We weave our dreams, we take a chance.
Each step we take, a guiding star,
Together bound, no distance far.

In silent nights, compassion grows,
A garden bright, where love bestows.
With every heart, we learn to care,
A tapestry of souls laid bare.

Through storms that rage, our spirits soar,
In unity, we find the core.
With hearts entwined, we face the day,
Illuminating paths of play.

Our laughter echoes, a soothing sound,
In every pulse, connection found.
With gentle hands, we mend what's torn,
In heartfelt care, new hope is born.

Developing a Garden of Earnest Feelings

In every seed, a promise waits,
To grow in love as nature creates.
We nurture dreams with tender hands,
In soil rich where hope expands.

A splash of color, a fragrant breeze,
Together we can plant such trees.
With patience, time, and gentle grace,
We find our blooms in this embraced space.

Each petal soft, each leaf a song,
In this garden, we belong.
Through seasons bright, through rain and shine,
We cultivate this love of mine.

In every flower, stories thrive,
A tapestry where dreams arrive.
With roots entwined, we learn to share,
Developing feelings, rich and rare.

Together we will tend and care,
This earthly path, a life we bear.
Through honest hearts, our garden grows,
In earnest feelings, true love shows.

The Delicate Balance of Affectionate Intent

In every touch, a world unfolds,
A dance of hearts, a tale retold.
With gentle words, we weave the night,
In delicate balance, pure delight.

The scales of give, the weight of dear,
Each act of care, our bond is clear.
Through moments soft, through laughter bright,
Affection blooms with inner light.

With careful whispers, we explore,
The depths of love, we long for more.
In every glance, a silent vow,
This balance cherished, here and now.

In shadows cast by doubt and fear,
We seek the truth so crystal clear.
With open hearts, we face the day,
This dance of love, come what may.

In currents strong, we find our way,
Affectionate intent in play.
Through trials faced, together we rise,
In delicate balance, love never dies.

Soundwaves of Shared Awareness

In murmurs soft, we hear the sound,
Of hearts aligned, where peace is found.
With every beat, a rhythm flows,
In soundwaves shared, our spirit grows.

With open ears, we breathe it in,
The music binds where we begin.
In harmony, our voices blend,
A symphony that knows no end.

Through tides of change, we stay awake,
In resonance, the bond we make.
With every note, we learn to trust,
In shared awareness, it's a must.

In quiet moments, wisdom speaks,
In every sound, our heart it seeks.
A gentle call, a tender plea,
In soundwaves shared, we're truly free.

Together we'll create the song,
In shared awareness, we belong.
With love as our unending guide,
In soundwaves true, we'll always ride.

In Full Awareness

Moments bloom beneath the sun,
Eyes open wide, our hearts run.
Every whisper a soft embrace,
Time suspended in this place.

Beneath the stars, we trace our dreams,
Caught in the flow of silent streams.
A symphony of thought and breath,
In this dance, no fear of death.

Feel the pulse of life around,
In stillness, peace can be found.
Every heartbeat, a gentle sound,
In full awareness, we are bound.

Hearts Adrift Together

Drifting softly in the night,
Our hearts soar, taking flight.
Waves of love wash over us,
In this moment, there's no rush.

Hands intertwined under the moon,
Lost in a timeless tune.
Every glance, a story untold,
In the warmth, we find gold.

Floating freely on this sea,
Two souls dancing, wild and free.
Adrift together, spirits twine,
In this journey, you are mine.

Artful Connections

Brushstrokes paint the dawn's embrace,
Every color finds its place.
In the gallery of our hearts,
Artful love, where life starts.

Canvas stretched, emotions flow,
In stillness, our passions grow.
Each laugh a note in harmony,
In this rhythm, we can be.

Echoes linger, soft and sweet,
In the moments, our souls meet.
Artful connections, like a song,
In this melody, we belong.

Attuned to Each Other

Frequency of thoughts align,
In the quiet, our hearts shine.
Every whisper, a gentle call,
In this rhythm, we feel small.

Eyes as mirrors, reflecting light,
In a world where all feels right.
Nature's song in our ears,
Washing away the doubts and fears.

With each heartbeat, we respond,
In this connection, we're both fond.
Attuned to each other's grace,
In this love, we find our place.

When Eyes Speak

In silence, words go unsaid,
A glance, a whisper, a thread.
Through shadows, love finds its way,
In every look, we dare to stay.

The twinkle tells a hidden tale,
A story where our souls set sail.
With just a gaze, the world ignites,
In silent realms, we chase the lights.

Each sparkle holds a memory bright,
A dance of stars in the velvet night.
With every blink, connection grows,
In unspoken love, our hearts compose.

The language of the heart unfolds,
In glances that our fate beholds.
Echoes linger in the space,
When eyes meet, there's an embrace.

So let them speak, the eyes that shine,
In every gaze, your heart is mine.
For in this world, where words may fail,
Together, we weave our endless tale.

A Journey of Gentle Steps

With every dawn, we take our stride,
The path unfolds, side by side.
Each step a note in our sweet song,
Together we know we belong.

The whispers of the morning dew,
Guide us to dreams, both old and new.
Through valleys deep and mountains high,
We'll chase the sun across the sky.

In gentle winds, our hearts will dance,
Embracing fate, we take the chance.
Hand in hand, we'll face the unknown,
In every moment, love has grown.

Together, we share both joy and tears,
Through laughter bright and lingering fears.
A journey rich, a tale we write,
With gentle steps, we'll find the light.

As stars align and shadows fade,
In memory's embrace, our love is made.
And when we pause to catch our breath,
We'll cherish every step till death.

The Heart's Compass

In every beat, a tale unfolds,
A secret path that love beholds.
Guided by whispers of desire,
A compass set, we'll never tire.

Through tangled woods and rivers wide,
Our hearts align, no need to hide.
With every choice, the journey flows,
The map of love is all we know.

In laughter shared and sorrows borne,
The compass spins—our love reborn.
With every trial, we find our way,
And in each heartbeat, come what may.

The heart's compass knows no bounds,
In gentle moments, it resounds.
We follow the line that leads us true,
With every pulse, I'm drawn to you.

And when the stars light up the sky,
The heart's compass will never lie.
For in its dance, we find our fate,
Together, we celebrate.

Beneath the Surface

In still waters, secrets abide,
Ripples whisper, truths collide.
Beneath the wave, the world is deep,
In silent depths, our promises keep.

The surface shimmers, a fleeting glare,
Yet in the quiet, we feel the care.
With every tide, a story flows,
In hidden realms, our longing grows.

We dive into the ocean's heart,
Where dreams and fears are set apart.
In shadows cast, our spirits dance,
Amidst the depths, we take our chance.

Ebbing waves, they pull and sway,
Leads us where the echoes play.
In every splash, we're intertwined,
Beneath the surface, love is kind.

So let us sink into the blue,
Where the unknown will guide us through.
For in that depth, we find our place,
Beneath the surface, we embrace.

Threads of Connection

In the loom of life, we weave,
A tapestry of souls, we believe.
Colors blend in our shared fate,
Every stitch tells love innate.

In laughter's echo, bonds are found,
In silent moments, hearts resound.
Through joy and tears, we're intertwined,
In every heartbeat, truth defined.

Paths may twist, but roots hold strong,
In the dance of time, we belong.
Though miles stretch, threads taut remain,
Connection flourishes, love's sweet gain.

Through storms that test, we stand tall,
Each whisper shared, a sacred call.
In the fabric of our days,
Together always, in countless ways.

When shadows fall, we light the way,
In unity, we find our stay.
Threads of connection, timeless and true,
Forever sewn, me and you.

Whispered Hopes and Dreams

In the quiet night, wishes soar,
Carried on winds, forevermore.
Each star a beacon, bright and bold,
Whispers of futures yet untold.

With every heartbeat, hopes ignite,
In the canvas of dreams, pure and bright.
Visions of laughter, love, and peace,
A tapestry where worries cease.

Under moonlit skies, we dare to dream,
In the silken shadows, possibilities gleam.
With faith as our compass, we will find,
A world where dreams are unconfined.

Each whispered prayer, a gentle thread,
Woven through hearts, by kindness fed.
In the garden of wishes, seeds we sow,
Together we flourish, together we grow.

Through the silent hours, dreams take flight,
Guided by hope, they shine so bright.
In the embrace of the night, we believe,
In whispered hopes, our hearts perceive.

A Symphony of Affection

In tender notes, love's music plays,
Harmony sweet, in countless ways.
With every glance, a melody sweet,
In every touch, our hearts compete.

Strings of laughter gently twine,
Chords of trust, a love divine.
In the rhythm of shared delight,
We dance together, hearts alight.

Through highs and lows, we find our tune,
In the quiet hours, beneath the moon.
A symphony crafted, note by note,
With every heartbeat, love takes boat.

Together we soar, a joyful refrain,
In the symphony's pulse, joy and pain.
With echoes of dreams that never fade,
Our love, a song, sweetly portrayed.

In the concert of life, we stand as one,
In every verse, our love's begun.
A symphony of affection, endlessly clear,
In harmony's embrace, we hold dear.

Unveiling Quiet Devotion

In gentle gestures, love unfolds,
A tale of hearts, silently told.
In quiet moments, we find our grace,
In every glance, a warm embrace.

No grand displays, just soft-spoken vows,
In hushed affections, time allows.
With every day, devotion grows,
In simple acts, our love bestows.

Through life's routines, we weave our dreams,
In tranquil whispers, devotion gleams.
In the stillness, our spirits merge,
With every heartbeat, love's soft surge.

In the shades of dawn, promises bloom,
In the dance of shadows, love finds room.
Unveiling the beauty, subtle and true,
In quiet devotion, I cherish you.

As seasons change, our bond stays tight,
In the canvas of days, love's pure light.
In the silence shared, we've found the way,
Unveiling our hearts, come what may.

Threads of Intent in Every Touch

In every gentle brush, a story we weave,
Silent whispers linger, more than we perceive.
Fingers dance like shadows, soft upon the skin,
Each caress a promise, where love can begin.

Moments stretch like fabric, stitched with glimmered thread,
Echoes of affection, in the words unsaid.
Connections run so deep, through laughter and through tears,
A tapestry of memories, that chases all our fears.

Embraces hold the warmth, of all that we have shared,
In the quiet heartbeat, every soul's laid bare.
We find our strength in presence, a bond through every sigh,
With every heartbeat closer, we touch the infinite sky.

Colors merge and flow, like paint upon a dream,
In every single touch, life's intricate seam.
On this canvas of love, we sketch our heartfelt truth,
Threads of intent woven, in the fabric of youth.

With every passing glance, a universe unfolds,
In every silent promise, stories yet untold.
These threads become our legacy, in shadows and in light,

We'll carry them forever, through the day and night.

Sculpting Tender Moments

Beneath the open sky, our laughter takes its flight,
With every shared glance, we sculpt the purest light.
Fingers touch like rivers, tracing paths unknown,
In every fleeting second, our hearts are overthrown.

Moments softly gather, like petals in the breeze,
Each word a gentle chisel, each pause a soft tease.
We mold tomorrow's dreams, with every breath we share,

In the warmth of the evening, love fills the air.

Shapes of fond affection, created in the night,
Casting shadows of our love, shimmering and bright.
With each soft revelation, we carve away the fears,
Creating space for hope, through the laughter and the tears.

Tenderness like water, flowing strong and free,
Crossing all the bridges, in what's meant to be.
Every moment matters, like clay within our hands,
Together we'll shape magic, where the heart understands.

As time begins to whisper, our stories intertwine,
In the studio of life, where your heart meets mine.
We'll sculpt these tender moments, until our days are done,
In the gallery of memory, our masterpiece unwound.

Navigating the Depths of Care

In the currents of our thoughts, we drift from shore to shore,
Each wave a gentle whisper, beckoning for more.
The depths reveal the treasures, we hold within our hearts,

As we navigate together, where love's journey starts.

Through the tides of joy and sorrow, our spirits intertwine,

Every gesture speaks volumes, in a language so divine.
We learn to chart our course, through the storms that life may send,
Finding strength in unity, where love and hope transcend.

Every glance is an anchor, keeping us secure,
In this expanse of feeling, our connection feels so pure.
We dive into the silence, beneath the surface calm,
Exploring deeper waters, where our hearts can feel the balm.

With each stroke of kindness, we swim against the tide,
Creating waves of comfort, where the tender feelings hide.

Together we discover, the vastness we can share,
In the ocean of our care, we find our love laid bare.

As we sail through life's ocean, with stars that guide our way,
Navigating every depth, turning night into day.
With you, I feel the privilege of all that's yet to come,
In the depths of our devotion, forever we'll be one.

Notes of Sincere Devotion

In the quiet of the night, I pen my tender prose,
Each letter sings your name, as my heart overflows.
With every stroke of ink, I capture what we feel,
Notes of sincere devotion, strumming chords so real.

Whispers caught in paper, flutter like the leaves,
In the melody of moments, every soul believes.
The rhythm of our laughter, the harmony we share,
A symphony written softly, in a world laid bare.

With a gentle cadence, we dance through every year,
Turning pages of our story, bound by joy and fear.
Each note like a heartbeat, echoing the truth,
In this sacred composition, our love stays uncouth.

Together we compose, through the trials we embrace,
A legacy of memories, that time cannot erase.
With melodies of patience, we weave the threads of trust,
In the score of our affection, it's love that's truly just.

As I write this sweet refrain, with every word I speak,
You're the song inside my heart, the music that I seek.
In the chiaroscuro, where shadows lightly blend,
Notes of sincere devotion, that will never end.

The Light of Tenderness

In gentle whispers, hearts align,
A glow that softens every line.
In eyes that speak of warmth and care,
The light of tenderness is rare.

With every touch, a spark ignites,
Bringing comfort through the nights.
A hand to hold when shadows creep,
In tender moments, love runs deep.

Each word like silk, a soothing balm,
In chaos, it brings a soothing calm.
With every laugh and silent tear,
The light of tenderness draws near.

In shared embraces, solace found,
A pulse of joy, forever bound.
With open hearts, together we roam,
In the light of tenderness, we're home.

We walk the path with open eyes,
In every glance, a sweet surprise.
Together weaving dreams so fine,
In the light of tenderness, we shine.

Unwritten Stories

Pages blank, our futures hide,
In whispered dreams, we confide.
With every heartbeat, tales begin,
In unwritten stories, we win.

Moments fleeting, a fleeting glance,
In every chance, a precious dance.
As laughter echoes in the night,
Unwritten stories take their flight.

Through every trial, through every tear,
In shared whispers, love draws near.
With every chapter, life unfolds,
In unwritten stories, truth is told.

Together we write, with hearts so free,
In the ink of time, just you and me.
With every smile, new tales arise,
In unwritten stories, hope never dies.

Though pages fade, our love remains,
In every line, the joy, the pains.
Together, we pen a life divine,
In unwritten stories, our hearts align.

Sharing the Weight

In silent struggles, we confide,
With every burden, side by side.
Together facing the darkest day,
In sharing the weight, we find our way.

With every tear that falls like rain,
We lift each other through the pain.
In gentle words, a soothing balm,
In sharing the weight, we find a calm.

When shadows loom and spirits tire,
Together, we spark a hopeful fire.
In lifting hands, we banish fear,
In sharing the weight, we draw near.

No mountain too steep, no valley low,
In unity, our strength will grow.
With every step, new courage gained,
In sharing the weight, love is sustained.

As paths entwine, we journey on,
Through every dusk, through every dawn.
With hearts united, we'll always say,
In sharing the weight, we find our way.

The Canvas of Companionship

Brush strokes bold and colors bright,
In friendship's glow, we find our light.
Together painting dreams in the sky,
On the canvas of companionship, we fly.

Each moment shared, a vibrant hue,
With laughter's cadence, our spirits grew.
In every challenge, we find our voice,
On the canvas of companionship, we rejoice.

From whispers soft to shouts of cheer,
In every heartbeat, we draw near.
With every scene, memories blend,
On the canvas of companionship, love knows no end.

The brush of life, we wield with grace,
Creating beauty in every space.
With strokes of trust, we paint the day,
On the canvas of companionship, come what may.

In this masterpiece, our hearts displayed,
Through every shade, our bond conveyed.
With colors rich, forever we stay,
On the canvas of companionship, we lay.

Milton Keynes UK
Ingram Content Group UK Ltd.
UKHW021954151124
451186UK00007B/234